AS PER MY PREVIOUS EMAIL....

AS PER MY
PREVIOUS
EMAIL...

AS PER MY PREVIOUS EMAIL...

STEVE BURDETT

POP PRESS

2

Pop Press, an imprint of Ebury Publishing

20 Vauxhall Bridge Road
London SW1V 2SA

Pop Press is part of the Penguin Random House group of companies whose
addresses can be found at global.penguinrandomhouse.com

Penguin
Random House
UK

First published in the United Kingdom by Pop Press in 2020

www.penguin.co.uk

A CIP catalogue record for this book is available from the
British Library

ISBN 9781529107494

Design by Clarkevanmeurs Design
Project management by whitefox
Written by Steve Burdett

Big thanks to the following fellow e-correspondents reporting from the front line:
Charlotte Hotham, Graeme Thomson, Sam Bevans, Luke Carpenter, Liv Walmsley,
Ant Hill, Laura Bevan, Rebecca Bull, Laura Martin and Joe Chalmers.

Printed and bound in Great Britain by Clays Ltd, Elcograf S.p.A.

Penguin Random House is committed to a sustainable future for our business,
our readers and our planet. This book is made from Forest Stewardship Council®
certified paper.

Contents

Your inbox has almost reached capacity: Introduction

○ **Steve Burdett**

To: Reader

When asked, 'What do you do?', assuming we aren't ravaged by shame or desperation to impress, most of us answer with our actual job. 'Account manager'. 'Experiential Marketeer'. 'Entrepreneur'. But let's face it, most of us should just answer honestly: 'I answer emails all day.'

Other messaging tools come and go, but email has remained the immovable mountain of office comms. Its subject field, CCs (and BCCs, for the sneaky among you) tower above the clouds, its architecture unchanged since its first use in bulky white PCs in offices across the world. And, inevitably, email has developed its own language, its own set of customs to be observed, which, in the hands of some, have become finely poised passive-aggressive daggers to the heart.

This book will explain the most annoying and passive-aggressive expressions and etiquette used in work email culture, all learned from a career spent doing what I do: I answer emails all day.

I wrote this in the knowledge that I was guilty of almost every piece of email behaviour I describe in these pages. The 'hope you're wells', the 'just checking ins' – 'the nice to e-meet yous'. I'd even 'circled back' a couple of times.

Delete

Reply

Reply All

Forward

Attach

Junk

Move
Flag

They started to fill me with a hopeless dread. The humble exclamation mark suddenly felt like a weapon at my fingertips – one I had hitherto happily used to carpet bomb inboxes. But now I realised that lives were at stake – well, sort of – and, as a flood of unread and yet-to-reply messages saw my inbox groan towards maximum capacity, I realised I had the personal capacity to change. And if I can change, trust me, you can too.

Nobody ever lies on their death bed wishing they'd spent more time emailing at work. Nobody.

Life is short. Careers aren't forever. Copying in your boss to highlight the shortcomings of a colleague isn't going to warm the frostbitten wasteland at the core of your soul. You don't need to tell a complete stranger that you hope they're well. How the hell did 'best' become an acceptable sign-off?

Let's use the time we have to cut through the crap and communicate free from the perils of passive-aggressive asides and toe-curling cliché. Let's communicate IRL with the person sitting opposite you. Let's cut down on the silly abbreviations. Let's, you know, not be dickheads.

The future's at stake. Let's warm the core of our souls, one email at a time – even as the planet inevitably burns around us.

Regards,
Steve

Steve Burdett
e-Correspondent/author/human. Uber 4.42*. BA (Hons)
Please consider the environment before printing this email.
Sent from my iPhone

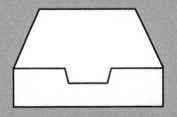

URGENT!!!

↓

Subject field stresses

It's the title of your missive, the name above the billboard that might spawn multiple sequels by way of reply. It's your email franchise. So why do so many subject fields leave us baffled, irritated and confused – and with no appetite for a sequel? It's the first thing anyone will see of a message in their inbox, so try to be pithy not pissy, please. But then again . . .

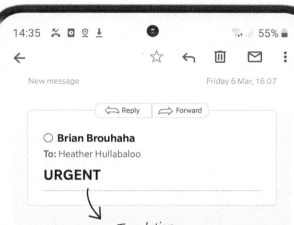

14:35 🕐 55% 🔋

← ☆ ↩ 🗑 ✉ ⋮

New message   Friday 6 Mar, 16.07

⟵ Reply   ⟶ Forward

○ **Brian Brouhaha**
To: Heather Hullabaloo

URGENT

Translation:
I know, it's not urgent at all. It's a month away! It's just pure workplace clickbait from yours truly.

> ⚠️ **EMAIL FILTER**
> If it isn't urgent, don't put 'urgent' in the subject line. It's desperate and attention-seeking. You know what happened to the boy who cried wolf? No one bothered opening his emails after a while, and then he had a client meeting that genuinely was urgent. OMG – disaster!

| Delete | Reply | Reply All | Forward | Attach | Junk | Move | Flag |

○ **Jess Tate**

To: Martha More

Will you be coming to next Friday's press event? I need to get numbers nailed before COP today, and haven't heard back from you. Let me know!!!

EMAIL FILTER

If you can no longer see the beginning of your subject field as you type it, if someone has to scroll through to read it, if you're forming complete sentences – hell, if it's any more than a handful of words, it belongs in the body of the email. Nobody thinks you're busy or eccentric. They think you're a tit. The only way this could be more annoying is if you had written it all in caps and used more exclamation marks.

Inbox

Message

Delete	Reply	Reply All	Forward	Attach	Junk	Move	Flag

○ **Heather Hullabaloo**

To: Brian Brouhaha

...

Translation:
The subject field is a minor inconvenience beloved by lesser mortals than my all-important self. OK, full disclosure: it's the only way I can get people to actually open my messages, the only sense of mystery in my grim and pointless existence.

EMAIL FILTER
Blank subject fields look weird. People feel blindsided walking into a message with no idea what's within. Would you read a book with a blank cover? Commence a ten-part Netflix series with no idea what it was? And for the more anally retentive types, it means they have to fill in the subject field themselves to file the email away. Anal people don't like that. Nobody likes that. Any of the subject-field no-nos in this chapter is preferable to none at all. Fill in the damn field.

| Delete | Reply | Reply All | Forward | Attach | Junk | Move | Flag |

○ **Brian Brouhaha**

To: Jess Tate

Are you busy?

Translation:

Now, am I asking because I suspect you're not and I'm interested in your reply? Am I asking because I'm genuinely curious? Or am I asking you because I want you to help me with something, and I'm a cold-hearted pass-agg arse who imagines putting you on the defensive will make it difficult for you to say no? Given that I'm your manager and I have a direct eye line to your desk, you've got to ask yourself a question: Is it going to be a yes, a no, or a heavily caveated yes that includes a description of all the work you're busy with but adds that you'd be more than happy to help, yes siree? (It's almost certainly going to be the latter.)

 Is there a more loaded question in the workplace? (Other than 'who made that mess in the men's **EMAIL FILTER** room?') And who would fancy typing a one-word reply in the subject field, 'yes', and then upping the pass-agg ante in a game of brinkmanship with no winner? If you want help or have some work for someone, make that clear, instead of inducing anxiety with your loaded gun to the head.

14

New message   Friday 6 Mar, 16.07

⟵ Reply   ⟶ Forward

○ **Heather Hullabaloo**

To: Jess Tate

Please call me.

Translation:

Knowledge is power. I know what I want you to call me about. You, however, could be faced with anything from the news that you're fired, or a chat about some minor issue at work or confirmation that your annual leave request is OK. The power is all in my hands, and the manner in which I choose to wield it is a symptom of the unbearable inadequacy I've felt since being a small unnoticed child.

> ⚠️ **EMAIL FILTER**
> We are all of us intolerant of uncertainty in the workplace. Don't make your every banal utterance a potential melodrama, and instead say what you want to talk to someone about in the message. Or better yet, call them your fucking self.

⟵ Reply   ⟹ Forward

○ **Heather Hullabaloo**

To: Jim Talent

Quick question

Translation:
Slightly misleading one here, as it almost certainly isn't going to be quick and rather than a question, it's more a request for you to do a whole heap of work to help me answer it. And guess what? No spoilers as to what this 'question' is about — you're going to have to open the email to find out. Drum roll, please!

⚠ **EMAIL FILTER** The subject field is a place to put the subject of your email. No one puts 'quick piece of information' or 'quick-to-download attachment' in the subject field. They say what the message is about. Simple, non?

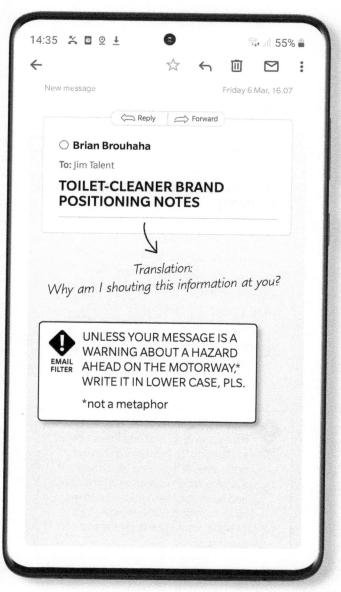

Reply   Forward

○ **Jess Tate**

To: Whole company

MARTHA'S LEAVING DO ON FRIDAY!!!

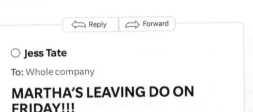

Translation:
I don't think capital letters are enough to grab your attention, so how about an exclamation mark? Wait, how about three? And if you think that's eye-catching, you should see the amount of exclamation marks on the reminder for our Monday morning Webinar — I like to bring the fun to work, let nobody tell you different!!!

EMAIL FILTER

No exclamation marks, please. Oh, it's a leaving do and you are actually exclaiming it? Then you get to use one – one. Never, ever send me your Monday morning Webinar reminder, and keep your fun where I keep my inner torment: bubbling quietly out of sight, until a few drinks in at a leaving do.

Message

| Delete | Reply | Reply All | Forward | Attach | Junk | Move | Flag |

○ **Brian Brouhaha**

To: Jim Talent

Reminder

Just a friendly reminder about the invoices you agreed to send over today.

↓

Translation:
Reminder? What kind of condescending pass-agg artist uses 'reminder' as a subject? And don't think saying it's a friendly reminder lessens its impact. It's about as friendly as a visit from a debt collector and— hang on. Those invoices. Shit. Forgot all about them — thanks for the reminder!

EMAIL FILTER

Don't scold a colleague like you'd scold a child. In fact, this is nothing like scolding a child because at least you'd be doing it to their face. Using 'Reminder' as a subject field is pass-agg scolding at its worst. Just say what the email's about instead of making clear the depths you're having to plunge by reminding us.

Delete   Reply   Reply All   Forward   Attach   Junk   Move   Flag

○ **Heather Hullabaloo**

To: Jess Tate

Re: MARTHA'S LEAVING DO ON FRIDAY!!!

Hi,
Did you have any joy getting the payroll data from accounts?
Thanks
H

To: whole company

From: Jess

Hi all,

Just a reminder that Martha's leaving do starts at 5.30 in the
Cape of Good Hope over the road. Free bar till 7 so get there pronto!

Look forward to seeing you all there,

Jess

*Translation: I'm so lazy I can't actually be bothered
to compose a new email, and thought I'd use an old
chain instead. I can't even be bothered to change the
subject, because what difference does a subject make
when we're getting to the heart of a matter, even if
that heart is something so deadly dull you might never
have opened it had it been in the subject field?*

Delete   Reply   Reply All   Forward   Attach   Junk   Move   Flag

EMAIL FILTER

One of the few kinds of recycling that isn't doing the planet any favours, using an old email chain for a new issue without changing the subject really pisses people off and makes you look either like a lunatic luddite who can't use email properly or the pass-agg cliché you really are. Change the subject. Compose a new email. But for God's sake don't come to me dressed in the sheep's clothes of a leaving do and then come over all wolf-like and ask for spreadsheets.

I CC You

↓

The pass-agg art of copying in

The CC field, used sparingly and appropriately, can inform and update colleagues and allow the wheels of business to turn smoothly. Of course, no one uses it sparingly and appropriately, or even knows how, so really it's an opportunity to pass the buck ('I'm CCing you because this is your problem'), stitch up your colleagues and cover thine arse, allowing the wheels to clog up on the grist of mutual distrust and hatred. Ah, sweet, sweet working life in the twenty-first century. CC is a weapon of pass-agg destruction that should require a licence, but in fact everyone has it at their disposal. And as for the BCC field, I've no idea what kind of sneaky sonofabitch invented this – it's for workplace psychos only.

Message

| Delete | Reply | Reply All | Forward | Attach | Junk | Move | Flag |

○ **Mike Hunt**

To: Steve Burdett
CC: Your boss, motherfucker

Friday Zoom

Can we set up a Zoom call between
you and me for Friday at 10am?

Translation:
*The workplace equivalent of a tattle tale, CCing your
boss in the first instance is the weapon of choice to tell
you: 'I don't trust you to do this properly without your
manager watching you.'*

EMAIL FILTER

Talk about getting off on the wrong foot. CCing
a manager in the first instance for something
that doesn't require their attention is a surefire
way to have the recipient going to Defcon 1
and readying their own weapons of pass-agg
destruction, spreading the word about what
a supergrass you are. Unless you have good
reason not to, prevent a slow-burning mutually-
assured destruction by trusting someone to do a
simple task in the first instance.

Message

Delete	Reply	Reply All	Forward	Attach	Junk	Move	Flag

○ **Kyle Renson**

To: Daisy Rey
CC: Daisy's Boss

Re: Medical cannabis focus group findings

It would be helpful if you could provide them, Daisy, and perhaps keep the tone more professional.
Thanks
K

From: Daisy Rey
To: Kyle Renson
Subject: Medical cannabis focus group findings
FFS Kyle, we're really swamped here. Can you not get hold of them yourself?
Daisy

Translation: Sucker! I've bided my time throughout this long and tiresome exchange, during which you have shown yourself to be incompetent and irritating. Now, when you've finally sent something unhelpful, I've applied the coup de grace, CC'ing your boss. You're shit, and now she knows you are.

EMAIL FILTER Timing is everything, and no more so than for the master of the pass-agg arts probing for a weak spot. And once they've suckered you, there's no way back. FFS, keep emails professional and to the point.

Message

Delete

Reply

Reply All

Forward

Attach

Junk

Move

Flag

○ **Daisy Rey**

To: Kyle Renson

FW: Medical cannabis focus group findings

Can you believe this prick?

From: Kyle Renson
To: Daisy Rey
CC: Daisy's Boss
Subject: Re: Medical cannabis focus group findings
It would be helpful if you could provide them, Daisy,
and perhaps keep the tone more professional.
Thanks

Translation:

So giddily high am I sending on a message slagging you off that I've accidentally sent it to you. Now I'm going to have to deal with this personally. Unless I can run to your computer and delete it before you see it.

EMAIL FILTER

Just . . . no. Don't become a workplace cliché. Keep it civil – not like a civil war – and deny yourself the short-term thrill of sending not-nice messages. Save the slagging off for the pub afterwards. Though that's almost certainly going to be within earshot of the target . . . Maybe WhatsApp is a good place to do it? Or not at all?

Message

| Delete | Reply | Reply All | Forward | Attach | Junk | Move | Flag |

○ **Mike Hunt**

To: Steve Burdett
CC: Your boss

FW: Monday Update

Just a reminder about the update I asked for . . .

Hi Steve,
Could I have an update on Monday's super-important
pitch, please?
Thanks
Mike

Translation:
Your failure to complete a task in the first instance,
necessitating a follow-up from me (how dare you),
has given me no choice but to discount laughable
excuses like you might be busy with other, far more
important things than me, and CC your manager in.
Please, please send me that update, though . . .

EMAIL FILTER

In baseball, a batter gets three strikes before they're out. They don't get an email with their coach copied in telling them off after the first strike. Give peeps a chance. In fact give peace a chance.

Message

| Delete | Reply | Reply All | Forward | Attach | Junk | Move | Flag |

○ **Kyle Renson**

To: Daisy Rey
CC: Mike Hunt; Daisy's Boss

Medical cannabis samples.

Hi Daisy,
Can you please return the promotional cannabis samples you borrowed? Mike and your boss copied in for information/sight.
Best
Kyle

Translation:

So passive is my personal brand of pass-agg that I feel the need to point out the fact that I've copied in the boss in the body of the message, thus making me an OK kind of guy/ gal after all. Am I right? Also, don't you dare just hit 'reply' now — I've upped the stakes to 'reply all'.

> **EMAIL FILTER**
>
> On the one hand, thanks for the head's up. On the other, it's just a head's up that you're a weak-willed tell-tale tit. Unless it is absolutely necessary – and if it's your micromanaging ball bag of a boss asking you to CC him on all your correspondence then it's time to have a quiet word – don't copy in the boss. Give peeps a chance (I'm hoping this will catch on).

New message

Reply   Forward

○ **Mike Hunt**

To: Kyle Renson
CC: Every man/woman and his/her dog

Our weekly 121

Translation:
I like to keep my arse covered, even if it's a conversation just between the two of us really, and it's coming at the expense of any long-term prospects in the workplace as colleagues quickly tire of my attritional CCing and soon learn to discount anything that pops up in their inbox under my name.

EMAIL FILTER   Sure, keeping people in the loop is a noble ambition in theory, but in reality *we hate you*. Who wants to waste time opening messages that have nothing to do with them? That's several seconds of life we'll never get back. Taken over the course of a career, you could be talking about years. Stop robbing life and start living yours.

Reply | Forward

○ **Kyle Renson**

Reply all: Mike Hunt
CC: Every man/woman and his/her dog

Re: Our weekly 121

Translation:
If it wasn't already annoying enough that you've been copied into a huge group email, I've decided to hit reply-all rather than a simple reply, so that you can continue to be bombarded with messages. There's no going back after a reply all.

! EMAIL FILTER Does every person on that email need to read your response? There's a handy button near Reply all. It's called Reply. Give it a whirl, you might just like it.

14:35

New message

Friday 6 Mar, 16.07

Reply | Forward

○ **Kyle Renson**

To: Daisy Rey
BCC: Mike Hunt

Mike's pitch notes

Translation:
I am one Machiavellian motherfucker.

> **EMAIL FILTER**
> This makes the serial CCer a person of great honour and compassion by comparison. Perhaps there are good reasons to use BCC, but surely only the most perverted pass-agg persecutor would consider its use all fair in love and workplace politics.

Message

 Delete   Reply   Reply All   Forward   Attach   Junk   Move   Flag

○ **Mike Hunt**

To: Jon Gent
CC: Every man/woman and his/her dog

Adding CC back in . . .

From: Jon Gent

To: Mike Hunt
CC: Just some men/women (no dogs)

From: Mike Hunt

To: Jon Gent
CC: Every man/woman and his/her dog

Translation:

So you felt the email chain was getting a bit crowded, maybe you felt some of the people on it really didn't need to see something so irrelevant to their job? Well, guess again, friend. I've added them back in. And if you take them off again I'll just do it again. And again. And again.

 EMAIL FILTER You're the kind of unblinking nightmare unlikely to lose a game of pass-agg chicken any time soon, but ask yourself why must these people be copied in? Do all recipients really need proof of the daily banalities of your job? Does the person taking them off have a point?

New message

Friday 6 Mar, 16.07

Reply | Forward

○ **Kyle Renson**

To: Jon Gent
CC: Daisy Rey

Missing medical cannabis samples

Just copying in Daisy, who should be able to help.

Translation:
This is not my problem. I'm CCing you to make damn sure it becomes yours.

> ⚠ **EMAIL FILTER** Dropping a colleague in it might make for a brief feeling of stimulation that other humans call pleasure, but it's all too fleeting. Perhaps actually asking the person concerned instead of CCing without warning might help resolve whether they actually can help. And maybe you could resolve to get your kicks elsewhere. Have you thought about BDSM?

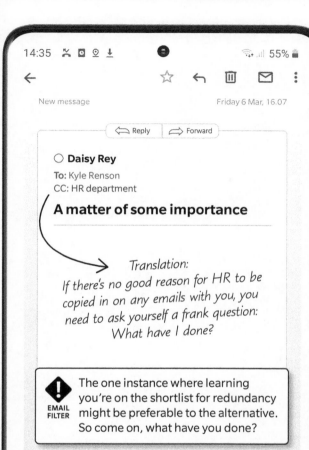

Salutations!

Putting the Hell in hello

Saying hello at the start of a message should be a simple matter, but thankfully a combination of workplace etiquette, extreme narcissism, petty grievances and power struggles mean it's actually fertile ground for any self-respecting e-correspondent to sweat over. Is 'hello' too informal for a job application? Does 'salutations!' make me sound like the 'bit of a character' I imagine myself to be? Is it possible to skip this part of the test?!

Send | Reply | Reply All | Forward | Attach | Junk | Move | Flag

Dear Penny,

Translation:
I've got my formal attire on, which might lead you to believe this is a stranger from a far-off, glass-fronted corporate entity pitching business to you. In fact it's Elsa. I sit at the other end of the office. We've worked together for years. And keeping you at arm's length allows me to deliver suitably pass-agg emails to you with a clear conscience. Frosty? Moi?

> **! EMAIL FILTER**
> The 'dear' was culled with the advent of email. Anyone who thinks writing letters and writing emails are closely related disciplines needs to put the quill down and pick up an iPhone. They're distant cousins at best, and you can bet Email dreads having to sit anywhere near Letters at family gatherings. Try a 'Hello'. You might find it's exactly what you've been looking for.

← Reply   → Forward

Hi Penny!

Translation:
Hello! I never listened at school when they explained what exclamation marks are for and I can't stop exclaiming everything!

 EMAIL FILTER You had the perfect salutation – Hi Penny – and then you had to spoil it all by using something stupid like an exclamation mark. Do you imagine it makes you sound sunny and upbeat? You're wrong! You're annoying! Stop it!

⟵ Reply   ⟶ Forward

Penny,

Translation:
I've dispensed with the pleasantries and gone curt, which could either mean I'm a bit narked at you and this is how I vent my truth, or I'm a straight-down-to-business kind of guy/gal and this is how I get down to business. My weekends are invariably bare and lonely affairs.

⚠ **EMAIL FILTER** Any greeting that sounds more like an admonishment is a no-no. You're not ticking off an unruly child – even if it might feel that way – so at the very least, grit your teeth and smuggle in a 'Hi'. Don't you feel better now?

Send Reply Reply All Forward Attach Junk Move Flag

Hey Steve

Translation:
So, like, I'm just totally relaxed, almost horizontal, you know, and just thought I'd see how you're doing. Oh, and also could you have those spreadsheets to me by COP today?

EMAIL FILTER
Look, a 'hey' can lazily roll off a Californian's tongue like it's the coolest way to greet someone ever, but that doesn't mean we then acquire the right to use it from our desk in a strip-lit office in Peterborough.

⟵ Reply   ⟹ Forward

Hey there

Translation:
I would not greet you so informally and yet so anonymously if I had any respect for you. Or even knew who you were.

⚠ **EMAIL FILTER** Sounds like a bad chat-up line, invariably reads even worse as an email opening. File under never, ever use.

Send | Reply | Reply All | Forward | Attach | Junk | Move | Flag

Jen passed on your details as she said you might be able to help with the copy for our launch on Monday. Let me know if you can rise to the challenge and we can talk further.

Best,

Jim

Translation:
I've dispensed with greetings because I'm a businessman and I'm a busy man and don't you go wasting my time if it isn't all about the business and . . . yeah, I'm a rude prick.

 Failing to address the recipient in the first instance, *especially if it's the first time you are ever*
EMAIL
FILTER *emailing someone,* is exhibit A in a trial that will see you found guilty of possession of zero social skills. It just looks weird and makes you seem hostile. And you're a pussycat really, aren't you?

Reply · Forward

Hi guys

Translation:
I am a patriarchy-pusher. Someone get HR on the line.

EMAIL FILTER

While 'guys' may be seen as an acceptable gender-neutral term for some, that doesn't mean everyone will be OK with it. And besides, anyone who calls a group of people 'guys' is unlikely to be worth spending any time with IRL. Am I right, guys? You could try 'folks' if you don't possess any self-esteem, but for the rest of us how about 'Hi everyone'?

Reply   Forward

Morning all

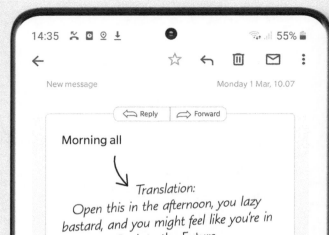

Translation:
Open this in the afternoon, you lazy bastard, and you might feel like you're in Back to the Future.

EMAIL FILTER

Wishing me a good morning when I read it in the afternoon feels like a perfectly pitched pass-agg snark about the fact that I'm not reading your emails in the part of the day you imagined I would. And if that's the case, I'll start opening them *the following morning*.

Reply | Forward

Hello mate

Translation:
I'd rather drink directly from the urinals than ever go for a drink with you, 'mate', but that's not going to stop me using patronising and insincere expressions to get what I want from you. OK, buddy?

> **EMAIL FILTER** Spare us the faux-matey bantz, 'friend', and leave your pally honorifics for your real friends – assuming you know how to identify who they are in your life. (Spoiler alert: you might not have any.)

'Hope You're Well'

↓

And other pointless opening lines

You never get a second chance to deliver an opening line. Well, you do – in the very next email you send. But that's not to undermine its importance in setting out the comms style of brand You. Whether it's the heart-sinking three-letter salute 'FYI', a bit of faux-bonhomie or an icy pass-agg rejoinder to a perfectly innocent request, it's a veritable minefield that you'll want to navigate safely as quickly as possible. So you can get on to the next minefield in the message . . .

Send

As per my previous email . . . |

Translation:
At what point did you decide that actually reading emails was optional? And at what point did I become so passive-aggressive that I can actually feel my middle finger burning up your screen?!

EMAIL FILTER — Leave the passive-aggression in your fingertips and simply repeat what you need to repeat. Then look outside. Isn't it a beautiful day? You work in a windowless office. OK.

New message

Send

Hope you're well! |

Translation:
Your existence means nothing to me.

EMAIL FILTER It's banal but harmless, and admit it: you couldn't care less. Why waste your time typing it? And for the love of God, what's with the exclamation mark?

Send | Reply | Reply All | Forward | Attach | Junk | Move | Flag

Nice to e-meet you! |

Translation:
I am as socially inept and cliché-spouting
in the flesh, too!

> **EMAIL FILTER**
> When was the last time you made a phone call and said, 'Nice to tele-meet you'? Did people waste valuable time with this shit back when they used telegrams? You aren't meeting them, you're sending an email. 'Hi' and their name is more than enough to stop you sounding like the bored and disingenuous desk jockey they'll eventually discover you are anyway.

New message

Friday 6 Mar, 16.07

 Send

Just circling back . . . |

Translation:
I will hound you to the ends of the earth.

EMAIL FILTER

You can give it any name you like, but pestering is pestering. And saying you're 'circling back' – or even worse, that you intend to circle back soon – makes you sound like a stalker. One whose vocabulary is composed entirely of workplace cliché.

New message   Friday 6 Mar, 16.07

◁ Send

Sorry for being unclear . . . |

↓

Translation:
Stamping it repeatedly into your forehead
would not have been as clear as I was,
you moron.

⚠ EMAIL FILTER And so we come to a the pass-agg apology, the 'sorry but not actually sorry at all, dipshit' that has been known to make grown men and women cry tears of mirth and frustration and satisfaction as they type it. But if you're not sorry and you weren't unclear, don't waste your time saying you are. Save your apologies for the many occasions you'll inevitably need them at work. Starting with your behaviour at the Christmas party . . .

Message

Send	Reply	Reply All	Forward	Attach	Junk	Move	Flag

Just floating this to the top of your inbox . . . |

Translation:
I'm pestering you, natch, but through cloaking it
in my amazing powers of levitation and presumption
I'm telling you exactly where I rank my request in
both your inbox and your to-do list.

EMAIL FILTER There's no quicker way to see an email fall from the peak of the pile than through some pest presuming to tell you they've put it there. All you're telling them is that you know how to send an email. And they can see that already. So just get to the point.

$\searrow$ Send

I thought I had sent this but it was sitting in my drafts . . . |

Translation:
This and other tall tales are available from my litany of excuses to cover my late replies and ineptitude.

EMAIL FILTER The 'dog ate my homework' of email excuses when a simple apology for being late would draw a line under proceedings – and not leave the recipient rolling their eyes at your BS.

Send   Reply   Reply All   Forward   Attach   Junk   Move   Flag

As per our conversation, here are the points you've agreed to address by the end of the week. |

Translation:

So we did it the old-fashioned way, had a good old face 2 face, IRL convo, mapped everything out beautifully, but then I thought I'd follow up by putting it in writing, copying in a couple of other people and very firmly put the ball in your court while dangling a sword above your head and totally mixing my metaphors. We simply **must** *do the old face 2 face again soon.*

EMAIL FILTER

Any message that begins with 'As per' is immediately going to rankle, especially if you've already talked everything through in person – not just the old-fashioned way, but the WAY OF THE FUTURE if any of us is ever to derive any kind of actual happiness from our work. Unless it was agreed when you spoke or you're dealing with someone so unreliable that they demand this kind of treatment, there's no need to spoil IRL conversations with your version of events in handy note form.

New message   Friday 6 Mar, 16.07

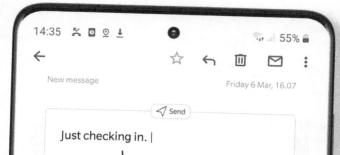

◁ Send

Just checking in. |

Translation:
I'm pestering you, plain and simple.

EMAIL FILTER A fave of the pusillanimous pass-agg pest, save your check-ins for the airport if you don't want people to give your requests a fly-by.

Send   Reply   Reply All   Forward   Attach   Junk   Move   Flag

I don't know about you but 2020 is FLYING by for me . . .
Hope you're enjoying the sunny weather we're having. |

Translation:
There is a void deep in me that can only be filled by
endless, pointless, tiresome small talk — you should hear
me chat to automated answering services — and the
cleansing salty wash of my own tears.

EMAIL FILTER Glib opening bullshit from people you've never met. Do these people have a random crap-opening-quote generator for their emails? Say hello, get to the point – spare me your pontifications on the fleeting nature of time or the fucking weather.

New message

Friday 6 Mar, 16.07

⊲ Send

Just reaching out to you |

Translation:
I'm writing an email to you to ask you something, a fact you are no doubt aware of thanks to the presence of an email from me in your inbox asking you for something. But do you feel the image of my arms outstretched from beyond the screen enhances my request? Do you?

EMAIL FILTER You sound about as human as a 'you have been in an accident' call. Spend less time reaching out to your keyboard to type this redundant rubbish and you might find people believe you're a real boy or girl.

Send Reply Reply All Forward Attach Junk Move Flag

I'm running a 5k for charity and hope you can sponsor me – here's a link to my JustGiving page. |

Translation:
I wear a halo and I'm pretty sure I'm your hero. You will be judged mercilessly on your contribution.

EMAIL FILTER

The great eye-roller of inbox intruders. Oh, sure, you're a great person. Doing an event that just about anyone whose organs and limbs were in functioning order could manage with zero training and only a little effort. A marathon? Maybe that's more worthy. But even then are you the type to train hard and run your best time or do you think walking large parts of it over 6 hours somehow warrants my dipping my hand in my pocket? Yes, it's for a good cause, but unless you're doing something that demands real effort – an ultra-marathon in the Sahara, watching the entire collected series of *Friends* in one sitting without sleep – you're opening yourself up to derision. Happy to contribute to the good cause, I'm just not going to be shamed into it in the name of your feeble efforts.

Send   Reply   Reply All   Forward   Attach   Junk   Move   Flag

Just checking you received my last email, as I don't seem to have heard from you. |

Translation:
I know you got it. You certainly know you got it.
Now can you politely reply to me, dickhead?

EMAIL FILTER

A stone-cold classic from the pass-agg archives. Don't rise to the bait and allow yourself to point out the multitude of other reasons that would involve them not hearing from you, such as the fact that you hate them.

That's great, thanks. |

Translation:
My response to just about any message. Go on, try me. 'That' could actually be anything from great, to utterly unremarkable and mediocre, to a huge pile of shit.

EMAIL FILTER Were true greatness to land in an inbox, surely no one would waste such a vapid, meaningless adjective like 'great' upon it. Purge it from your e-lexicon and let's make email great again.

Send

Can you send me the email again? |

Translation:
I think we both know it's either in my deleted items or inbox, but surely you can't expect me to go to the trouble of taking my eyes from my Insta and actually looking for it.

EMAIL FILTER
These lazy mouth breathers might not value your time, but are you really valuing your own if you then contact IT and investigate the Case of the 'Missing' Email in order to expose their lies and bring them to justice? Resend with the minimum of fuss (leave out the 'here it is again' if you can help it), and if you haven't already, file the recipient under 'Moron'.

Message

Delete

Reply Reply All Forward Attach

Junk Move Flag

○ **Jim Talent**

Friday 6 Mar, 16.07

To: Lucy Look

FW: The Meaning of Life

Thoughts?

✉ > Re: Message forwarded
✉ > Message forwarded
    ✉ > Re: Message forwarded
    ✉ > Message forwarded
        ✉ > Re: Message forwarded
        ✉ > Message forwarded
            ✉ > Re: Message forwarded

Translation: Rather than waste precious minutes of my own diminishing lifespan summarising the nightmare email chain below — which would be easily done given that I've been a part of its 100-messages-plus existence — or even indulging in some simple pleasantries or basic sentence structure, how about you spend the afternoon trying to work out what any of this even means before you let me know what you think, so that I then know what I think.

> ⚠ **EMAIL FILTER**
> If you are going to ask someone to shovel shit for you, at least dress it up in a prettier package; one that isn't going to leave the recipient dreaming of stoving your head in with her company laptop.

Delete	Reply	Reply All	Forward	Attach	Junk	Move	Flag

○ **Jon Gent**

To: Mike Hunt **cc:** Lucy Look

Client meeting

Hi Mike,
Just looping in Lucy ...
Regards
Jon

Translation:
Hi Mike, you narcissistic, petty Hunt,
Just reminding you that Lucy exists. You know, sits opposite
you, is your only direct report, does most of your work for
you (buttering up the blue-chip clients with an avalanche of
bullshit and company-sponsored booze aside, of course) . . .
I hate you.

> ⚠ **EMAIL FILTER** While 'looping in' might conjure up images of lassoing the moral high ground, not to mention valiantly defending/patronising beyond belief those who have been forgotten on the message, don't get cocky. It's a slippery slope towards the diabolical dickheadery of the I CC You chapter.

14:35   55%

← ☆ ↰ 🗑 ✉ ⋮

New message   Friday 6 Mar, 16.07

 Send

Can you ping me on Slack? |

Translation:
Needlessly asking to move the conversation onto another medium from this perfectly adequate one. Yes, I know exactly what you're thinking: Gofuckyourself . . .

 EMAIL FILTER If you're the sort of person who does this, it might already be too late for you.

 Send

Happy Friday! |

Translation:
Living for the weekend means I'm dying
all week long.

! **EMAIL FILTER**

While we're all grateful for you celebrating the day of the fucking week with us, if your message is about to stop us knocking off early for the weekend then it is certainly not going to be a Happy Friday unless we're dangling you by your ankles from the 15th floor. And don't ever wish anyone a Happy Monday. Unless it's a Bank Holiday.

Direct Mail

↓

Getting to the point already

It says everything about the way we email that it's Chapter five before we actually get on to the body of the message. And if you thought the waters had been choppy up to now, they've got nothing on the tsunami of abbreviations, acronyms, desperate corporate jargon and tired old workplace cliché threatening to drown us all. In fact, there's enough corporate jargon going round to fill a book on its own (note to self: email publisher re: 'idea for Book 2'), but thankfully there'll be no puppy-punching, thought showers or running anything up flagpoles in this chapter. We don't really need to explain why you're a massive wanker for saying things like that, do we?

◁ Send

It would be a huge help if you could be flexible on this.

Translation:
Change your mind, motherfucker.

⚠ EMAIL FILTER   A pure pass-agg pearler in the suggestion that by not acquiescing to your demands, the recipient is being both unhelpful and inflexible, but it cuts both ways: you're also suggesting your powers of persuasion are copy and pasted from *The Idiot's Guide to Workplace Cliché*. And you might need something more like a Jedi Mind Trick to convince them otherwise.

◁ Send

Thanks guys, we love it. Just a couple of points to incorporate for the next round.

Translation:
We hate it. Junk what you've done and do this instead.

⚠ EMAIL FILTER
Don't say you love it when you hate it and want everything about it changed. You're not softening the blow; you're allowing the wound from your blow to fester, possibly becoming gangrenous. Be diplomatic by all means, but don't be such a disingenuous dipshit.

Send

We need to manage expectations going forward.

Translation:
The client has an idiotically unrealistic picture in their head that needs downgrading fast. You're going to need to kiss some serious arse if you don't want me to kick yours.

EMAIL FILTER

Face it, you mean lower someone's expectations, and dressing it up in this pass-agg nonsense guarantees you've fallen well short of everyone's rock-bottom expectations.

New message

Friday 6 Mar, 16.07

Send

Do you think maybe we could . . .

Translation:
Meh meh meh meh ... are you still reading this hesitant, weak, sugar-coating bullshit?

EMAIL FILTER — Putting a traffic jam of hesitant and indecisive expressions at the start of your request doesn't make you sound more pleasant or polite. It makes you sound like an insipid wallflower. So maybe in future, I mean if it's not too much trouble, do you think you could possibly, I don't know, just fucking ask for what you want?

Send

Can we PLEASE make sure we have everything by close of play TODAY?

Translation:
I am CAPITALISING these words for EMPHASIS, blissfully unaware that there is a FUNCTION called italics that might sound a fraction LESS like I am SHOUTING them.

EMAIL FILTER
Can we please make sure we have everything by close of play today? Look, it still makes perfect sense. And it doesn't read like a letter from a serial killer. Winner.

Send

Going forward, let's do this.

Translation:
Let's start doing this from . . . now! And keep doing it for ever or until I either forget about it or have more ideas that we will need to assimilate 'going forward'.

⚠ EMAIL FILTER Nothing sounds more backward than someone 'going forward'. It's a completely redundant thing to type. Given that time flows only one way outside of sci-fi films, which other way might we be going? Sideways? I thought that was the direction of your last 'promotion'.

Send	Reply	Reply All	Forward	Attach	Junk	Move	Flag

Let's make sure we're all singing from the same hymn sheet.

Translation:
We'd all better be on message or there will be
some serious repercussions.

>
> **EMAIL FILTER**
>
> In a godless world it's tempting for some to get all teary-eyed and nostalgic for institutions who, at one time, were more than happy to crucify those who weren't 'on message'. Save your pass-agg propaganda and say it clear and simple for the believers and the non-believers alike.

Send   Reply   Reply All   Forward   Attach   Junk   Move   Flag

Could the person who keeps putting food in the recycling bin please stop?

Translation:
*Ever have a flatmate who would leave notes on the fridge asking everyone not to drink his or her milk or to try aiming at the toilet bowl in the bathroom once in a while? Well, that's me, and now I've got mail! And while I **know** it's you unthinkingly dropping the remnants of your takeaway Nando's in the recycling bin, I couldn't very well just come out and politely ask you not to, could I?*

EMAIL FILTER
Actually, you could. As long as you didn't come off sounding like the condescending oxygen thief you almost certainly are.

Could you let me know the key takeaways from the meeting?

Translation:
Life for me is a set of listicles, a constantly refreshing BuzzFeed column that ensures I have my finger on the pulse. Just the edited highlights for me: the Match of the Day to a live football match, turkey without the trimmings, the trailer to the film. Actually go to the meeting myself? Me? You're having a laugh!

EMAIL FILTER

Constantly asking people to write up the crux of things – or key takeaways, if we're slumming it in your jargon-heavy depths – is lazy, entitled dipshitery at its worst. Your colleagues are not listicle-writing diarists of office life – leave that to the pros, please – they've also got jobs to do. Go and ask them about it if you have to.

Send	Reply	Reply All	Forward	Attach	Junk	Move	Flag

Let's touch base offline.

Translation:
Can we meet up and talk, like, face to face?
You know, actually IRL?

> **! EMAIL FILTER**
>
> There is a vast unknowable world called 'offline', a place fewer and fewer of us are prepared to set foot in, which leaves no lengthy message chain and renders many favoured email pass-agg asides irrelevant, but it is one we must venture to if we're to save humanity. Though we must not 'touch base' there, for that is the language of idiots. And we must not call this world 'offline', for it is the grass/tired carpet/minimal-styled concrete beneath our feet, and the sky above our heads (well, about seven floors up and above the roof, at any rate). Fancy a chat in the place they call the café?!

Sorry to be a pain, but would you mind . . .

Translation:
Not sorry. Happy to hold you in a choke hold until either you get this done for me or you breathe your last.

> **!** **EMAIL FILTER** 'Sorry to be a pain' inevitably means you're going to be a massive one. Everyone knows that. Leave out the meaningless pass-agg apology and get straight to the point.

← ☆ ↰ 🗑 ✉ ⋮

New message   Friday 6 Mar, 16.07

⟨ Send

Please cascade this information to your teams.

↘

Translation:
Conjure up your frothiest inner waterfall and, er, tell the people who need to know this. Bearing in mind that you're all downstream from me, hierarchically speaking.

⚠
EMAIL
FILTER
While you might imagine you're implicitly asserting your position in the hierarchy through saying 'cascade' instead of 'share' or 'tell', what you're explicitly doing is asserting your status as a cliché-spouting robot.

I don't have the bandwidth to take this on, I'm afraid.

Translation:
I'm too busy, I'm not doing it and you can't make me, so there.

> **⚠ EMAIL FILTER**
>
> One day, when your job has become automated and you stand shivering in the queue for the post-apocalyptic soup kitchens of the future (former Pret a Mangers), people will look back and declare the original author of this expression the Nostradamus of office life, predicting the rise of the machines. In the meantime, however, they should be lynched, along with anyone else caught using it. Say you're busy, say you're swamped, but don't be a cyborg.

Send Reply Reply All Forward Attach Junk Move Flag

To kick off, I'd better tell you I've had to move the goalposts on this project, so the ball is in your court and I'll need revised offers by close of play today.

Translation:
The only thing I love more than sport is sport metaphors. And the only thing I love more than that is shafting people like you by changing the rules to make life easier for me and, of course, more difficult for you. You do like sport, right?

>
> **EMAIL FILTER**
>
> People who don't like sport are unlikely to enjoy sport metaphors when you're shafting them. Nor are people who do like sport, for that matter. There's no court and certainly no 'play' in this office, so don't call the end of the day that. Otherwise I might have to kick off with you.

⏳ Send

FYI, Jen is WFH today. IMO we should obvs push on – agree? LMK by COP.

BW,

MH

Translation:
For Your Information; Working from Home; In My Opinion; Let Me Know; Close of Play; Best Wishes; Mike Hunt ... ITBTTP: I'm Too Busy To Type Properly.

EMAIL FILTER
You can't reduce everything to its initials, no matter how hard you try. Erase confusion overnight and stop your emails reading like a teenager's messaging app through the simple practice of typing what you want to say and leaving the superfluous crap in your vacant head.

Send

Sorry, I'm going to have to send this back your way, as it falls under your team's remit ;-)

Translation:
Schadenfreude tastes delicious when it's delivered through a fuck-you winky face.

EMAIL FILTER No emojis in emails ever, especially to deliver anything so smug and pass-agg – their use immediately shows you to be the least competent and most unpopular person in the workplace. What, you didn't know that? Oh, sad face ☹

Send

Teamwork makes the dream work as the saying goes.

Translation:
Here's a nice workplace proverb which should make up for the mountain of crap I've asked you to work through.

 EMAIL FILTER The kind of phrase that makes even the most liberal among us disappointed that guns are so hard to come by and the only knife in the kitchen doesn't even cut through butter. Using this expression should be an instantly sackable offence, and anyone on the receiving end should be granted six months' compassionate leave on full salary.

XXX

Awkward sign-offs and signatures

There might be Hell in hello, but you just try saying goodbye on email. People have wrestled with sign-offs since the beginning of time – or the 1990s, if we're being pedantic – some of the leading e-thinkers and men of virtual letters among them, and the best they have come up with is some version or another of 'Best'. That's not to say there aren't loads of equally terrible alternatives, of course, and email might be the only version of communication in which a kiss isn't even a kiss, it's just an 'x' that marks the spot where all sorts of trouble can start.

And that's before we even get onto the tricky politics of signatures. An e-sig is the equivalent of a business card, but if *American Psycho* was remade as a movie for the modern workplace, there would be no scene involving a bunch of banker psychopaths getting competitive over their e-sigs. And that's because e-sigs are shit. Yet somehow, with the same pioneering spirit that has seen humans dismantle the planet in the name of progress and grand delusion, people continue to conspire to make them even shitter.

New message   Friday 6 Mar, 16.07

☆ ↩ 🗑 ✉ ⋮

◁ Send

Hope this helps!

Translation:
*For the love of all that is right and holy in
this world, just leave me the hell alone now.*

 EMAIL FILTER Is saying 'hope this helps' actually
helping? You're only going to get
more irritated when they don't take
the hint and reply asking for more . . .

Send

Happy to discuss.

Translation:
Now get the fuck off my patch.

> ⚠ **EMAIL FILTER** There are better ways to draw a full stop to proceedings. Such as, you know, the full stop at the end of the preceding sentence.

Send

Let me know if that doesn't make sense?

Translation:
It makes perfect sense and I am terminating this conversation, dipshit.

EMAIL FILTER Applying some pass-agg pressure might pull up your drawbridge to all but the thickest-skinned dissenters, but you have invited the more literal-minded among them to storm your battlements and leave you furious with their lack of understanding or, let's face it, your lack of sense.

New message

Send

I will leave it with you.

Translation:
This is your job and you have exceeded
your allotted assistance from yours truly.
Sayonara, motherfucker.

EMAIL FILTER Deliciously passive aggressive and final in tone, you're unlikely to win friends and influence people but hey, Be Kind is a bumper sticker and at least no one is going to bother you with follow-up messages.

Thanks in advance.

Translation:
You have no choice now because you have already received my thanks. Played you like a fiddle there, sucker.

 EMAIL FILTER Fuck you – in advance.

New message

Send

If you have any questions, don't hesitate to let me know.

Translation:
I'm now officially ghosting you.

EMAIL FILTER

Yet another sign-off designed to tell the receiver 'piss off and leave me alone' (is there any other kind, really?), you're inviting trouble with invitations to interrogate you. Spare us and spare yourself this pointless expression.

⊲ Send

Look forward to hearing from you.

Translation:
Get back to me soon if you know
what's good for you.

⚠ EMAIL FILTER The kind of passive-aggressive bullshit that was as prevalent during the quaint letter-writing days of yore as it is today, and as equally annoying and ineffective now as it was then. I look forward to consigning this expression to the waste-paper bin of history.

⊲ Send

Kind regards,

Translation:
I have no idea what this means, but who cares? It's just an email to you. And seriously, who cares about that?

⚠️ **EMAIL FILTER** Genuine kindness is a disease and this expression is the cure. Has anyone outside an email ever used the expression 'kind regards'? Don't wade into its meaningless, cold depths and steer your sign-offs towards warmer waters. Though FFS don't think that's an endorsement for 'Warm Regards' – urgh!

| Send | Reply | Reply All | Forward | Attach | Junk | Move | Flag |

Best,

Translation:
I once agonised for hours over the best way to sign off an email, and this is the best I came up. It is the only time the word 'best' has ever been in such proximity to my name.

> **EMAIL FILTER** Wishes? Regards? All the best? 'Best' makes no sense and yet is possibly the most common email sign-off, and what's worse, people blindly accept it as being inoffensive and 'professional'. It's the worst, is what it is. It's best to give best a swerve, unless your second choice is 'Laters'.

New message

Friday 6 Mar, 16.07

Best wishes,

Translation:
I am a walking greetings card.

EMAIL FILTER

Unless you want to sound about as warm and sincere as a Hallmark production line, keep your best wishes – along with your hugs and kisses – offline.

Message

Send

Reply

Reply All

Forward

Attach

Junk

Move

Flag

Best regards,

Translation:
Simply the best, yeah! Better than all the rest
of my regards. Better than any of them . . .

It's official: there is no way to sign off an email that isn't entirely lacking in sincerity. If you can't beat them – and you can't, unless you want to resort to 'Ciao!' or something equally unbearable – then you might as well stick to the classics. All the best, zzzz . . .

EMAIL FILTER

Friday 6 Mar, 16.07

Send

Thanks!

Translation:
*I'm thanking you whether there is reason
to or not — my thanks know no limits and
seemingly have no end. Exclamation mark
optional, but I just LOVE IT!*

> **EMAIL FILTER**
> Save your thanks for when someone
> deserves it, not as a way for signing off
> every piece of correspondence. It's a
> pity 'sorry' hasn't been popularised as
> a sign-off for people who use this.

Send   Reply   Reply All   Forward   Attach   Junk   Move   Flag

Cheers,

Translation:
We're clinking proverbial glasses, buddy, in this informal 'thanks', even though I have nothing to thank you for and we've never met.

EMAIL FILTER — This might – *might* – be an acceptable way to sign off with a friend, but it's uncomfortably ingratiating when it's from someone you barely know. And if you're using it with a British colleague just stop. It's demeaning, for you and for them.

S

Translation:
My mantra: always sign off emails
with my initial to prove I am busier
than the recipient.

> **! EMAIL FILTER** You're fooling no one by skimping on the time-consuming letters that make up the rest of your name, 'S'. Yes, people who don't know you will see your name in your signature (please tell me you have one), but your ludicrous Zorro-like flourish to sign off will already be indelibly embedded in the recipient's mind. And they won't be thinking 'masked hero', trust me.

No sign off.

Translation:
CALL ME RUDE, CALL ME CURT, QUERY
WHETHER MY MESSAGE IS INCOMPLETE,
BUT DON'T MAKE ME SIGN 'BEST' OR
SOME OTHER BOLLOCKS AND MY GOD
DAMN NAME THAT YOU KNOW WELL
ENOUGH BY NOW AGAIN.

EMAIL FILTER

There is a cold logic to this, which only falls down when some recipients wonder if the message was sent unfinished and others think you're a rude prick. Or you're pissed off at them and you're a rude pass-agg prick. Unless it's people you know well, a sign-off in the first message at least is a must. Unless some compassionate leave on a workplace-trauma counsellor's sofa is in order?

Send

Humourless GiFs at the end of 'fun' work emails

Translation:
*If a picture paints a thousand words, then this **moving picture** only paints one: LOL! You're welcome.*

EMAIL FILTER

Usually found in the 'fun' emails from the self-appointed resident office 'joker', it's best to just smile politely and not encourage this kind of behaviour. You can always howl into the abyss on your lunch break.

Send | Reply | Reply All | Forward | Attach | Junk | Move | Flag

Nat Wood
Senior Civil Servant / Department of Work and Pensions / BSc

Translation:
I think I'm flexing my intellectual might in an office where, it turns out, the minimum job requirement is a university education.

EMAIL FILTER

If you've got an MBE, possibly. A PhD, maybe. But the presence of your lower second Batchelor's degree from a former Poly in your signature, in a subject completely unrelated to your job, is embarrassing, and will soon lead to much sniggering about a mysterious colleague known as 'the professor' while you carry on blissfully unaware.

Send

John James
Experiential Marketeer / SpamCorp
j.james@spamcorp.bot
[no phone number]

Translation:
I like to hide behind the curtain of written correspondence and rail against the conformity of e-sig ubiquity. This is really going to piss you off when you need an answer fast and you can't call me.

EMAIL FILTER

Thanks for putting your email address in your signature. Not sure how I'd have replied otherwise. *And yet you left off your phone number?* What are you hiding, you control-freak weirdo? No one likes having to go PI and spend all of two minutes tracking you down and then scrawling your number on men's room walls all over town. No one. But do it we must.

New message

⊲ Send

Sent from my iPhone

Translation:
The sender shall not be liable for any misunderstandings, major screw-ups or loss of personal reputation arising from the content and spelling herein because, hey, how can I be expected to read through something I've typed on a purpose-built messaging device with a screen so small it's too big to fit in a pocket and a spell-checker as standard?

EMAIL FILTER This isn't a get-out clause; it's a get-out-my-inbox offence. You can remove this notification in your device's settings. Do it. Do it now.

Message

Send Reply Reply All Forward Attach Junk Move Flag

Steve Burdett
Facebook: SteveBurdett
Twitter: Angry_Steve
LinkedIn: StevenJBurdettBSc
Instagram: BigFunStevieB
Slack: HipsterSteve
Zoom: EveryoneelseisdoingitsowhynotSteve
Pinterest: Isthisstillgoing?_Steve

Translation:
While I might work for a faceless corporation in an instantly forgettable field, check out my personal brand and get to grips with the kind of free-spirited individual I really am. Oh, come on — at least give my Insta a peek! 27 likes and counting on my last post.

EMAIL FILTER

It certainly seems strange to give anyone you email access to all the avocados you've ever posted. And are you fishing for a job, because why would they need your LinkedIn profile? Unless twitter or some other platform is relevant to your work (in which case have this handle only), one is almost always too many – though, to be fair, they do offer the opportunity to have a good laugh at your expense.

Send | Reply | Reply All | Forward | Attach | Junk | Move | Flag

Please consider the environment before printing this email.

Translation:
Yay, the environment. Stop cutting down trees for the sake of my words! Am I virtue-signalling enough for you? I did meat-free Monday once, though. And I have a reusable coffee cup (unused on my desk).

EMAIL FILTER

A bit like asking someone who's going to the shop to get you a sugary pick-me-up to use a reusable shopping bag. Fuuuuck, you! Everyone knows you're just trying to feel morally superior about the environment without actually having to do anything about it. And if you're the kind of technophobic dinosaur who is actually printing emails and compiling dossiers on colleagues, check what decade it is.

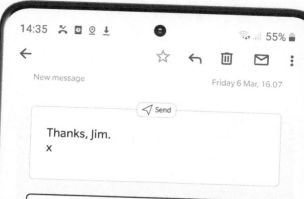

New message

Friday 6 Mar, 16.07

◁ Send

Thanks, Jim.
x

EMAIL FILTER No HR department has ever intervened because someone didn't put a kiss in an email, and this is one part of e-etiquette in which all manner of confusion, embarrassment and (on the flip side) flirtation and romance can arise. If in doubt, don't put a kiss at the end of a work email.

Double-O Nothing

When your Out Of Office
gets out of hand

An automated response to inform people sending you mail that you're away from work for a while. What a handy, straightforward solution that seems. But then again . . . will one's narcissism allow a template OOO to play assistant to brand you? Or are we crying out for something, well, just a little more you, darling? And what if the person I ask you to contact in my absence does a better job than me? And FOMO alert: what if something spectacular happens while I'm away – should I even bother having an OOO? Oh, this is a fucking nightmare, isn't it?

Send   Reply   Reply All   Forward   Attach   Junk   Move   Flag

The Oversharing OOO

Hi! Thanks for your message. I'm afraid I can't respond, as I'm on a silent retreat in Laos until the end of March with limited access to the trappings of modern life. Don't take my silence personally, and let's pick up when I return.

Namaste!

Esther Chance,
Prolapse PR

Translation:
It isn't enough for you to know the dates I'm unavailable. I simply have to brag about what I'm doing while you're stuck at your desk. And guess what? It's fucking amazing, a deeper journey into the self than that time my OOO told you I went on vegan safari in Botswana. And sure, it might be a 'silent' retreat, but that won't stop me chattering endlessly about it on Insta and, inevitably, replying to your email within a matter of minutes, as I simply can't bear the idea of anything in my life carrying on blissfully without me.

EMAIL FILTER   Anything beyond the dates you are out of the office and someone to contact in your absence is information you're desperate to impart but which no one wants to receive. Look inside yourself – why this shameless need to paint your life in such a way?

Send   Reply   Reply All   Forward   Attach   Junk   Move   Flag

The minute-by-minute OOO

I'm in meetings between 2 and 4pm this afternoon, but will reply to your message ASAP afterwards.

Jem x

Translation:
This place would fall apart if I wasn't on hand to reply to emails immediately 24/7, so just hold the phones, buckle up, and I'll be back soon to save this place with a prompt reply. You know I've got you on this one.

> **! EMAIL FILTER** Does anyone really need to know your movements in such detail? Is there anything that really can't wait an hour or two for a reply? Pull yourself together and ditch the minute-by-minute out of office. You'll feel less like you're being held to account by a higher power and the recipient won't think you're quite so full of your own self-importance.

Send Reply Reply All Forward Attach Junk Move Flag

The No OOO

Hi Esther,

I've emailed you a couple of times this morning and came to your desk this afternoon to follow up – only to learn you're in the middle of a week off. It's no biggee, but an OOO would have saved me a fair bit of time. Maybe something to think about next time.

Have a good break!

Best,

Gail

Translation:

I am clinging to my job by my chewed-up fingernails so desperately that I check my emails relentlessly even when I'm on holiday. It's all fine! Really, it's fine! Out Of Office is for wimps (and those with reasonable job security).

 EMAIL FILTER Give yourself a break and bite the OOO bullet. You'll feel better for it. Unless you're a freelancer, of course, in which case you can never, ever use an Out Of Office in case you miss out on some work. Welcome to your new normal.

Send | Reply | Reply All | Forward | Attach | Junk | Move | Flag

The 'I'm a real character, me' OOO

I'm drinking margaritas all day long on the coast of Mexico until 25 March. While I have ample access to internet and phone, I think we can both agree it would be best if I waited to reply when I returned.

Gracias y buenas noches!

Translation:
Everyone in this office is too polite to take me to one side and explain how patently unfunny, unprofessional and annoying I am.

EMAIL FILTER

What happened to the good old days when people would try to keep their drinking problems a secret? Just stick to the facts and leave the jokes to comedians (who almost certainly don't use OOO) and chroniclers of annoying email expressions (who are self-employed and wouldn't dare use an OOO for fear of missing out on work).

The Boilerplate OOO

I'm out of the office from 4 to 14 August, with limited access to email.

Translation:
This inbox will remain unread till
I'm back, bitches!

EMAIL FILTER

The OOO itself is ample explanation without this lame expression. Unless you're spending ten days on Mars, where the WiFi is famously patchy, no one thinks you have 'limited access to email'. They think you're on holiday. Which is allowed. In fact it's even a legal requirement of your job. Ditch the limited access and give it to them straight (calling them bitches = optional/potentially career suicide).

| Send | Reply | Reply All | Forward | Attach | Junk | Move | Flag |

The Pick Your Colleagues wisely OOO

I'm out of the office until 15 September. If your query is urgent please contact Esther Chance on . . .

Translation:
You need to break the glass and hit the emergency alarm button to justify contacting my colleague. And trust me, I haven't picked my most competent one to show me up while I'm away.

EMAIL FILTER A bit of a passive-aggressive guilt trip. That email you need a reply on within two weeks: is that really *urgent*? That seems an excessive description, doesn't it? But then you do need an answer, so you'll inevitably open your email to the colleague with: 'Sorry to bother you in Zara's absence, *but . . .*' And so the pass-agg cycle continues.

Message

| | | | | | | | |
| Send | Reply | Reply All | Forward | Attach | Junk | Move | Flag |

The OOO as No No No

I am on holiday with my family from 15 to 24 March. Any messages received during this time will not be read and will be deleted, so if it's important please get in touch again from 25 March. In fact, the message you've just sent will self-destruct in five seconds . . .

Translation:
I'm the kind of maverick who likes to return from holiday with an inbox as clear as my conscience. Kiss my arse, spambots and serial CCers!

EMAIL FILTER

An OOO sure to provoke outrage in many people receiving it. But come on, who wouldn't want to be like this? It takes guts and a refusal to look back to do this, qualities so far out of the average pass-agg pugilist's sphere of experience as to be truly exotic. And you know what? If it is important, you'll send it again. You might CC his/her manager when you do, you sad and envious little person, but you know you will.

Message

Send — Reply — Reply All — Forward — Attach — Junk — Move — Flag

Afterword: Recall This Message?

○ **Steve Burdett**

To: Reader

I wrote this book during lockdown in 2020, an 'unprecedented' time that promised to change the way we work for ever and demonstrated how quickly expressions like 'stay safe' could become insincere and annoying email cliché. But while scientists were busy modelling and monitoring the progress of a very physical disease, I was busy using wholly unscientific, anecdotal evidence to record the spread of something sinister in the emails of the imprisoned working population.

Gone were the opportunities to simply ask the person opposite a 'quick question' instead of sending a needless email (subject: 'quick question') and unnecessarily clogging up another inbox. Out went the meet-ups: the coffees, the lunches, the drinks with disastrous consequences after work (or during it). In came the kind of neuroses only working alone at home for weeks on end can engender (trust me, I've been doing it for years), with the opportunity to misread, misconstrue or simply analyse to death every little expression in written correspondence in lieu of some actual IRL interaction. (When we weren't sprucing up our homes for video calls, that is.)

In short, never had a guide such as this been needed. But if we're going to warm the core of our souls one email at a time, even as the planet inevitably burns around us, it really shouldn't matter if we're confined to a one-bed flat for the next decade or we're in a spanking new shared workspace. Because our mantra should remain the same no matter what: Don't be a dickhead.

Email is a difficult medium to master. You start a job and the expectation is that you're fluent in what is effectively another language. No one offers you any official training in the do's and don'ts. How are we supposed to know we shouldn't finish all our messages with a great big winky emoji and a shower of kisses? But now that you've read this book (you haven't just flicked to the back, have you?), you know what's, if not right, then certainly unbelievably fucking annoying.

I've typed so many of the pass-agg clichés and trite terms in this book throughout my many years on the frontline of e-correspondence that it fills me with the same shame I once felt as a boy when my mother asked me what I was doing while I was taking a sneak peek in one of her Jackie Collins novels. But, just as I quickly slammed the book down, went furiously red and said, 'Nothing!', so you too can seamlessly style out your past indiscretions and start sending messages that sound like a new human being. Or as close to it as you can manage.

Only send the message – if you have to send it – to the people who need it. A handful of words in the subject field – the fewer the better – that accurately sum up the content of the

Send

Reply

Reply All Forward

Attach

Junk

Move

Flag

message. 'Hello' or 'Hi' and the recipient's name. Get to the point with what you want, but *be polite*. Avoid workplace cliché. BE KIND, but not in capital letters. Sign off … actually, I still have no fucking idea what a good way to sign off is. Your name. A short signature with pertinent details, which is not in Comic Sans and does not contain a picture, especially one that moves. A clear conscience when you press 'send'.

Is this too much to ask?

I want you to imagine that, every time you hit the send button, you are effectively pressing your own self-destruct button (5, 4, 3, 2, 1 … BOOM!), and that email will be your last words, the epitaph on your headstone. A sobering thought for those of you who like to email on the toilet. Do you want those words to be snarky and passive-aggressive? Or do you want them to reek of the worldly wisdom of an e-Renaissance type who helped save humanity? And, come on, do you really want social-media handles on your headstone?

All of which leads me to here: how on earth do I sign off a book when I've yet to find a decent way to sign off an email? Best? Regards? Thanks? Ciao?!

Keep typing, you beautiful, monstrous emailers.

x